Habits of a Cheerful S

How to Master Your Thoughts to Create Positive Actions

Mental Toughness, Think Happy Thoughts, Affirmations

Michael Clarke

CONTENTS

INTRODUCTION

Take a moment to reflect.

Are you more of a glass half-full or half-empty kind of person? Do you look for the good in every situation, or are you more likely to focus on the negatives? Do you identify more with the eternal optimist, or the eternal pessimist?

It's easy to get bogged down with the stresses of life. From the moment you wake up, you're looking at the news, reading emails, organizing your packed schedule. There's stress coming at you from all angles, and it builds up over time. If you don't have a healthy way to manage all of life's stress, you're going to find yourself burnt out and miserable.

Fortunately, there is an easy and effective tool that will help you avoid all of that—positive thinking.

Positive thinking won't fix all your problems overnight; it won't cure you of your depression; it won't make all your deadlines disappear; and it won't stop you from feeling stressed. However, positive thinking will give you the tools you need to better manage stress and live a longer, healthier life as a result.

You'll be pleased to know that positive thinking isn't rocket science. There are many simple ways to start changing your mind to become a more cheerful place. You might want to start every morning with your list of affirmations, or maybe a few minutes of quiet meditation. Perhaps you'd prefer to boost your mood with a smile and a laugh, or surround yourself with positive people and bask in their cheerful glow.

Whatever you do to improve your mindset, you'll be happy to know that positive thinking won't only make you a more pleasant person to be around but teach you how to manage the struggles that life throws at you. Positive thinking will teach you how to cope with the stress of everyday living and give you the skills to improve your health for years to come.

If that sounds good to you, then you've come to the right place. Sit back, get comfortable, and get ready to learn how you can live a positive, healthy life from the comfort of your own mind.

First, we'll touch on the health benefits of positive thinking and show you exactly why you want to start doing it. It's not an exaggeration to say that a more optimistic mindset might actually make you live longer, there are real, scientifically proven physical benefits to positive thinking. We'll talk about a few key ways to become a positive thinker, giving you plenty of options, so you can figure out what best suits you. Whether you're interested in meditation, affirmations, or enjoying a good laugh, there should be something that will suit anyone and fit into any schedule.

Next, we'll discuss how the mind works. We'll talk about the conscious, subconscious, and unconscious minds, and how you can use positive thinking to influence all parts of the brain. With a little practice, you can train your subconscious mind to be more optimistic, using positivity to help shape you into a more cheerful person. We'll talk about the idea of neuroplasticity, or how to rewire your brain to be better at positive thinking. Plus, we'll touch on the importance of hormones like oxytocin, dopamine, serotonin, and endorphins, and how you can help keep them balanced to ensure an efficient brain.

Finally, we'll talk about how you can combine positive thinking with a healthy lifestyle so you can spend the rest of your life thriving, not just going through the motions. It's all about looking after yourself, physically and mentally. You are, after all, a physical being, and it's important to look after all aspects of your life. We'll talk about the importance of being proactive, why we procrastinate, ways to manage your mental health, and how much exercise you should aim to get on a daily basis. There's more to being a positive thinker than your morning affirmations.

By the time we're finished, you'll be ready to go out and tackle the world with a brand new mindset. You'll have the tools to find methods of positive thinking that work for you and learn how to incorporate them into your life to facilitate life-long benefits. No matter where you are now, these are the lessons that you'll want to carry with you throughout your life to help you thrive.

The first step towards becoming a positive thinker is easy: want to change. Judging by the fact that you picked up this book, it's safe to say that you've already achieved step one. Now that you're here, it's time to get started.

BECOMING A POSITIVE THINKER

L et's face it, the world isn't always the nicest place. It's filled with stress and worry, and it can be easy to let that weight get the best of you. But, if you want a simple, easy tool to help better yourself, you need look no further than the power of positive thinking.

If you're still on the fence about whether positive thinking can actually help you, you might be interested to know that the benefits of positive thinking can be seen physically. One study looked at data from more than 70,000 people over several years and found that optimism was strongly linked to decreasing rates of death due to "cancer, heart disease, stroke, respiratory disease, and infection" (Kim et al., 2016).

Another study rated the emotional content of handwritten autobiographies by 180 subjects in their early 20s. Decades later, when these people passed away, researchers found a strong correlation between those who were more positive and those who lived longer (Danner et al., 2001).

Why is this? What actually happens between being a positive thinker and living a longer life? Unfortunately, we aren't entirely sure. There isn't a clear, obvious link from positive thinking to better health.

One theory is that positive thinking helps us better manage stress, a serious danger to our health. When we're stressed, we release the hormone cortisol, which helps us respond to the source of our stress. If you can manage stress quickly and efficiently, you can keep your cortisol levels at their normal levels and there's no problem. If you fail to deal with stress correctly, continuously having high levels of cortisol in your system, that's when you start to see issues.

Prolonged stress has an impact on all aspects of your life. Not only do you become tired and irritable, but constant stress can also be accompanied by physical symptoms such as aches and pains, changes in appetite, sleeplessness, more frequent illness, and even chest pains. In extreme cases, you even run the risk of developing Cushing's Syndrome—a disease associated with unhealthily high cortisol levels and accompanied by weight gain, slower healing, acne, decreased fertility, fatigue, high blood pressure, headaches, bone loss, and diabetes.

Naturally, managing stress is vital. Positive thinking is one of the best ways to control your stress levels. You don't need anything other than your own mind to think, and you can do it anywhere. If you're not sure where to start, here are a few ways to start incorporating a more positive mindset into your life.

How to Be a Positive Thinker?

It's easy to say that you're going to become a more positive thinker, but, without a clear idea of how to actually go about changing your mindset, it can be easy to get stuck before you've even started. Positive thinking is a little more complicated than simply telling yourself "I'm going to be more optimistic."

Fortunately, positive thinking can be found in a huge range of forms. It's simply a matter of discovering what's out there and figuring out how you can adapt those methods to suit you.

Affirmations

Affirmations are statements you make to bring your focus towards more positive things. They might be something like, "I am a talented artist" or "I am a valued member of my workplace." You can even use affirmations to build on things that you want to improve. For example, if you want to become more confident, think about times when you already showed great confidence and build on that. Tell yourself that you are already a confident person, and that you are capable of being even more so in the future.

Your affirmations can be anything you want. You don't have to share them with anyone. You might find it helpful to put them up on a sticky note on your bathroom mirror, or maybe save them on your phone to look through during your commute to work.

If you're feeling stuck, brainstorm the things that you know about yourself. Are you a good public speaker? Do you have a lot of self-discipline? Are you a fast learner? Are you creative? Take it as an opportunity to remind yourself of the things you're proud of, and don't be afraid to be proud of yourself. Pride might be a sin, but a complete lack of self-confidence doesn't help either.

Several studies have found a scientific basis behind affirmations. One study found that the body's response to stress can be reduced using affirmation (Sherman et al., 2009). Another found that affirmation can even be a way to avoid ruminating on negative results (Koole et al., 1999).

Reframing Negative Thoughts

If you spend every waking moment focused on bad things that have happened to you, of course you're going to feel like the world is against you. Unfortunately, there's no switch to turn off all negative thoughts and you'll still have them from time to time. But, rather than obsessing over these, take a moment to think about how you can reframe these thoughts and give them a positive spin.

If your boss sends back a piece of your work with a thousand things to change, then look at it as an opportunity to see where you can improve; a chance to make your end product even better. If you have to take your car into the shop and it'll take a week to fix, look at it as a chance to get out and explore your neighborhood on foot.

If your phone battery dies while you're out, think of it as a chance to disconnect from the internet and reconnect with the people around you. If you've been rostered for an unusually long work week, focus on the fact that you'll have an extra something to put towards your savings when your paycheck comes in. If you have to wake up painfully early to fit in your morning workout, take into consideration the fact that you'll be able to watch the sunrise.

In a lot of situations, there is good to be found. You merely have to know where to look for it, and, once you do, you might be surprised at how much there is to find.

Out With the Negative, in With the Positive

It's hard to be positive when you're surrounded by negative energy. If you find that your friends bring you down more than they raise you up, it might be time to reevaluate your connection to them. Everyone has bad days, but if your friends are nothing but constant negativity, then you're going to be soaking that up whether you like it or not.

If you know people that are unnecessarily pessimistic, it might be a good opportunity to have a chat with them and talk to them about their mindset.

They might not even be aware that it's something that they're doing, and they might appreciate a little nudge in the right direction. If not, then it might be time to cut back the amount of time you spend together.

As you cut out negativity, be sure to bring in some positivity. If you're friends with an eternal optimist, see what you can do to spend more time together. Find out how they stay as positive as they do, and maybe they'll be able to give you a few pointers. Even if you can't find out their life secrets, just being around them will probably make you feel better. They say that a good mood is infectious, and the same goes for a good mindset.

Practicing Gratitude

Take a moment to think about all the things in your life that you're grateful for, and write them all down so you can see them in front of you. You might be surprised to see how long that list is. We all have things to be thankful for, whether that's something as simple as being able to enjoy a hot coffee on a cold morning, or something as wonderful as being surrounded by friends and family that love you.

Practicing gratitude is something that you can do every day. Before you go to sleep, take a moment to think about the events of the day. What opportunities arose? What went well for you? What do you have to be thankful for? It can be easy to let these things pass by without acknowledging them, meaning we're prone to forgetting about all the good things that we have in our lives.

By thinking about what we have in our lives, rather than what we're missing, we bring the focus back to the positive. We don't need to be famous or overwhelmingly wealthy to live happy, fulfilling lives. When you take the time to be thankful for the good in your life, you will likely find that there's plenty there to be grateful for, and it's important to regularly reflect on this to keep it at the forefront of our minds.

Meditation

Meditation is something that might sound intimidating at first, but it's actually pretty simple. You don't need to do it for hours, a few minutes can be beneficial. All you need to do is find a comfortable spot that works for you; perhaps lying in bed, sitting at the dining table, or even looking out over your garden. Close your eyes, if you need to, and focus on your breathing.

Try to forget about whatever it is that you're worried about, and keep your attention on your breath. If you get distracted, let it come, go, and then return to your breath.

When you're ready to stop, open your eyes and come back to yourself. Take a moment to reflect on how you feel. Are you feeling calmer? More relaxed? If so, that's great! If you're not feeling any different, that's completely fine too. You might find that, with more practice, you'll start feeling more of a difference.

Embracing Humor

You've no doubt heard the saying "laughter is the best medicine." Interestingly, there is actually a scientific basis to this saying. It has been found that laughter can strengthen the immune system, relieve stress, and even act as a therapeutic tool for illnesses such as depression (Seaward, 1992). And, even though there is a range of theories for why we laugh, research has shown that the benefits of laughter still apply, no matter which theory is used to explain it (Wilkins & Eisenbraun, 2009).

Don't be afraid to take some time to indulge in something silly. If you find a piece of art that makes you laugh, put it up on your wall where you can see it. If you come across an amusing picture online, save it and come back to it when you need a laugh. Spend time with your friends and share a few laughs. Creating humor in your life is the perfect little boost to add to a cheerful mind.

Being Kind to Yourself

Being positive isn't always easy. There will be times where thinking positively doesn't feel possible at all. When that happens, rather than getting frustrated because you're feeling negative emotions, try to cut yourself a little bit of slack.

If you get frustrated with yourself for feeling negative emotions, all you're going to do is make it worse. You're not a robot, of course you're going to feel bad from time to time. There isn't a person on the planet who is happy constantly. As long as you're making an effort, you're on the right track.

Learn to forgive yourself when you make a mistake. Nobody's perfect, and everyone makes mistakes. Learn to forgive yourself when you get stuck in a negative headspace. Sometimes, no matter what we do, we feel like garbage. In times of negativity, it might just be time to get a snack, put on your favorite movie, and wait for those feelings to pass. When it does, get up, dust yourself off, and keep going. The world isn't going to end because you had a bad day, don't treat yourself like it will.

Give Us a Smile

On one hand, if you find yourself in a particularly bad mood, you'll likely find yourself glaring or scowling—probably without consciously deciding to do so. On the other hand, if you're having a fantastic day, you'll probably find it hard to keep the smile off your face. A frown and a smile are common expressions that have very obvious meanings, and, it turns out, your body can recognize the meaning behind them without even needing to feel the emotion associated with them.

This is what is known as the theory of embodied emotions. Essentially, your body associates physical movement or body language with its respective emotion. If you frown, your body recognizes that this is typically associated with negative emotions, and, suddenly, you might be feeling a little bit worse than you were a moment ago.

Several studies have demonstrated this theory. One such study had subjects hold a pen in their mouth either between their lips or their teeth. When holding the pen with their teeth, subjects were forced to smile to keep their lips from touching it. The subjects who held their pens with their teeth, involuntarily smiling, reported a stronger "humor response" when presented with cartoons, compared with those who held their pens with their lips (Strack et al., 1988).

Similarly, a 2012 study by Kraft and Pressman had participants hold chopsticks in their mouths in ways that would force them to smile or maintain a neutral expression. Some participants were told to actively smile, while others did not have this mentioned to them at all. Researchers then gave the participants stressful tasks to carry out, and found that those with a smile (conscious or not) had lower heart rates than those with a neutral expression.

Another study found that people who had received Botox injections, and were consequently unable to frown, experienced fewer negative emotions and saw a reduced rate of depression (Lewis, 2018).

So, if you want to trick your brain into feeling a little bit lighter, don't be afraid to break out a smile. It might feel a little bit strange to smile before you've got anything to smile about, but it might give you that little boost your mind needs.

Finding Things to Look Forward To

What does your schedule look like for the next few days? Is there anything there that you're particularly looking forward to? Or, is it one long stretch of your regular, boring, old routine?

There's nothing better than having something to be excited about. Maybe that's coffee with an old friend, a trip away for the weekend, but, whatever it is, give yourself things to look forward to. It's hard to be negative when there's something good coming up in the near future.

Try to give yourself something to look forward to at least once a week. It doesn't have to be anything major; you could organize a stroll through your favorite local park or a visit to the weekend farmer's market. Just be sure to give yourself little treats throughout the week to keep your spirits up.

Journaling

The mind can be a pretty busy place, and it can be hard to keep track of everything happening without a little help. A journal is an excellent tool to help with organizing your thoughts, and there are multiple ways in which to utilize a journal to help promote positive thinking.

You could use it as a place to keep all of your negative thoughts. By transferring them to the page, you're essentially removing them from your brain. On the page, they can't cause you any more pain or stress and you've freed up more space for positive thought.

Alternatively, you could use your journal as a way to reflect on your day and process everything that happened. You might want to make a note of changes and fluctuations in your mood, and see if you can notice any patterns. For example, maybe you tend to get stressed whenever you visit a certain friend. Often, by writing things out as though you were explaining them to an uninvolved third party, it's easier to understand and make connections between things that you wouldn't have otherwise noticed.

You could also write about all the things you're grateful for, writing about all the things that you're happy about or your affirmations. It might be a little burst of happiness, here or there, or full of things you're happy and proud of.

The possibilities really are endless, and it's up to you to figure out what works best for you. Journaling, ultimately, is a great way to regulate your thoughts, keep track of your emotions, and remind yourself of your past, happy memories that you can use when you're feeling down.

Creating a Habit

Now that we know the benefits of positive thinking, and we have some strategies to create a positive mindset, let's talk about how to keep it up for the long term. Positive thinking is something that absolutely everyone can benefit from, and you'll get the most out of it if you engage with it on a regular basis.

If you've ever tried to set a New Year's Resolution, you've likely experienced the initial month of daily gym visits, juice cleanses, and regular vacuuming. As January comes and goes, and you find yourself settling back into your normal routine, along come the excuses.

It's too cold for my morning run, I'll just go tomorrow, you tell yourself. *I deserve a treat night, let's get takeaways*, you say. *I'll clean the house next weekend, I'm too tired now,* you complain.

If you want to make changes to better your life in the long term, you need to make sure that these changes become habits rather than something you pick up when you remember. If you want to see life-long benefits, you need to make sure that you're prepared to commit for the same amount of time.

At first, positive thinking might not be something that comes naturally to you, and that's completely fine. The important thing is that you find what works for you and you stick with it. It has been found that creating a habit can take anywhere from 18 to 254 days, but takes an average of 66 days (Lally et al., 2009). That means it'll likely take a couple of months of actively engaging in positive thinking in order to get it to stick. How you make a habit of positive thinking is completely up to you, but you need to find the type of positive thinking that works best for you and decide how to fit it into your daily schedule.

It might be a good idea to start with a few minutes of mindfulness at the start of your day. Start by writing out everything you need to do, or anything that's bothering you. Get it all down onto the page so you can see exactly what you're going to be dealing with. Then, maybe, spend a few minutes meditating or coming up with a plan for how you're going to tackle these issues.

If you're not much of a morning person, it could be helpful to do a little bit of positive thinking at the end of the day. You might want to do it as you're getting ready to go to bed. Put your phone down and take a moment to reflect on your day. It might be helpful to write out everything you need to do tomorrow or anything that you're worried about, and you can come back to it in the morning. Think about all the good things that happened in your day and what you're grateful for. Think about what you're looking forward to tomorrow, and what you're going to do to make it a great day.

If you do your best thinking during the day, try finding a few minutes here and there where you can practice some positive thinking. Maybe you'll do a little bit of journaling on your lunch break, or do some meditation before you head out for a meeting.

Once you know what works, set reminders for yourself. Maybe you'll set a daily alarm on your phone, or ask a friend to help keep you on track. You might want to leave written notes for yourself around your home, or you could set up a calendar with daily reminders.

Either way, it's all about reminding yourself until it becomes second nature. When positive thinking becomes a part of your daily routine, reminding yourself to be positive will become effortless.

Mental Toughness

Mental toughness is the idea of your mental strength, how much you can persevere when things get difficult. Being mentally tough means you'll have an easier time pushing yourself through struggles and achieving your goals.

Being mentally tough is helpful when it comes to forming habits. At the end of the day, you're responsible for keeping up the habit of being a positive thinker.

There isn't anyone else who is going to put in the hard work for you. If you don't keep pushing to make a habit of it, then no one will.

We all have a certain degree of mental toughness, and a study of elite athletes and their perception of mental toughness found three major ways to build and maintain mental toughness: "a desire and motivation to succeed that was insatiable and internalized, a support network that included sporting and non-sporting personnel, and effective use of basic and advanced psychological skills" (Connaughton et al., 2008).

Firstly, you need to really want to succeed. If you're on the fence about incorporating positive thinking, it's less likely that you're going to continue it in the long term. Take some time to really think about why you want to create a positive attitude, and make sure to remind yourself of this.

Secondly, you need a support network. Find friends that are interested in becoming more optimistic and get them on board. You can keep one another accountable while you're together. If they notice that you're being unnecessarily negative, they can help pull you out of it and vice versa. While it's true that your attitudes are ultimately up to you, that doesn't mean you can't accept a helping hand.

Finally, use the skills you learn. Use the methods of positive thinking that we've mentioned here, or go out and find your own. If you find something that works, stick with it, and make a regular habit of engaging with it.

CREATING A POSITIVE MIND

Now that we know a few different ways to go about being a positive thinker, let's delve into what's happening behind the scenes. Once we understand how our mind works, we can learn how to make it work for us and help us in our journey to becoming life-long positive thinkers.

Can A Person Dream Their Way To A Cheerful State Of Mind?

Dreams are a mirror to the subconscious mind. They are a way for the subconscious mind to communicate with the conscious mind fully. They can help to achieve goals. Sometimes dreams have people or things from the past in them. When this happens, people often wonder why. Perhaps there are unresolved issues with that person. Perhaps something recently reminded someone of that person.

Dreams are also a great example of the subconscious mind resolving complex issues. In dreams, people can often fly, achieve incredible feats that aren't possible in the conscious state of mind. Dreams are often the mind's way of dealing with things that the conscious mind either doesn't want to deal with or can't seem to find a resolution for during regular daytime hours.

Some people have recurring dreams where they have the same dream over and over. Sometimes in recurring dreams, they're trying to accomplish something or resolve a complex issue that they can't seem to resolve in their waking hours. Recurring dreams can also represent unresolved issues, and the mind is trying to resolve them.

Dreams can be representative of other things or issues going on in life and around it. They may be symbolic. There have been many studies on dreams and how they can affect people in their daily lives. How can they change things and outcomes?

Often a person will resolve a complex issue while they're asleep simply by focusing on the recurring dream. The mind's subconscious ability to find the resolution for complex issues is amazing. The subconscious mind acts like a storage unit of past experiences, memories, and solutions, all locked into the subconscious vault of the mind.

The subconscious mind is similar to a cloud on the computer. Here, everything is stored, neatly filed away for future reference. Even the most disorganized person will find that in their mind, everything is neatly filed away into compartments where they can later access important information and details, these are called memories.

Conscious, Subconscious, Unconscious

The mind exists in three parts: the conscious, the subconscious, and the unconscious. In many cases, the terms subconscious and unconscious are used interchangeably, but there are some subtle differences that are important to understand.

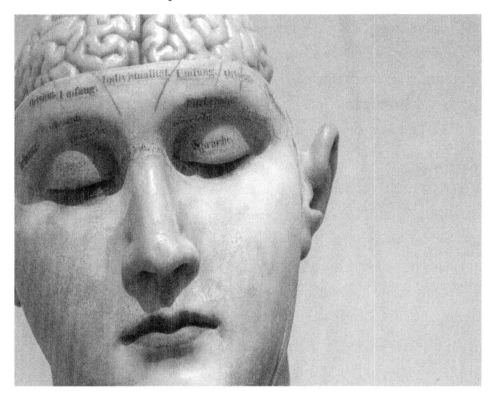

The conscious mind is everything you are aware of and can actively change. It's the thoughts that you're having, the decisions you're making. When you look at an empty mug and think to yourself, "oh, I should pick that up and take it to be washed," that's your conscious mind thinking and acting.

The unconscious mind is everything happening that you aren't aware of and can't consciously change.

It's the important, behind-the-scenes, technical activity, like your brain telling organs to function. You can't feel this happening, and you can't do anything to affect it.

The subconscious mind is the bridge between the conscious and the unconscious. Take your breathing as an example. Normally, it's completely unconscious, but, now that your attention has been brought to it, you're actively making your breathing happen. You can decide to breathe faster or slower, but, eventually, you'll forget and it'll go back to being an unconscious act.

The idea of a subconscious mind was popularized by the famous psychoanalyst, Sigmund Freud, and he likened it to an iceberg. The conscious mind floats above the surface, the subconscious mind just below the surface, and the unconscious mind deep beneath the surface. In fact, it is thought that the conscious mind only makes up 5% of the mind in total (E. Young, 2018). The vast majority of the brain is beyond our immediate control, but we can still influence it if we understand how it all works.

Influencing the Subconscious

A study related to implicit bias suggests that it is possible to influence what we believe subconsciously through mental imagery. Implicit bias is an "unconscious association, belief, or attitude" that we hold towards someone or something (Cherry, 2020). It's something that we pick up without even realizing, and it can often be in direct conflict with what we consciously think or believe. The study found that using mental imagery actively contrary to these biases is effective in reducing them (Blair et al., 2001). Those who used mental imagery that was neutral, in accordance with their biases, or who used no mental imagery at all, saw no reduction of their implicit bias.

The subconscious brain has no concept of right or wrong, it simply absorbs the information we present it. If we have a negative mindset, and constantly present it with negative information, negativity is what the subconscious is going to pick up. But, if we present it with a positive mindset and positive information, it will absorb and maintain positivity instead. Because the subconscious makes up the vast majority of our mind, having a positive subconscious is going to make it much easier to maintain a positive conscious mind and a positive life.

You have to consciously decide to be a positive person. You have to regularly and consistently present your subconscious brain with positive thoughts. You have to picture yourself positive and thriving, and you need to want to become a more optimistic person. It might take a bit of work, but, if we can turn our subconscious mind into a source of positivity, that is going to benefit us greatly in the long term.

The reason that we want our subconscious mind on our side is because it affects our behaviour in ways that we aren't even aware of. One study showed our lack of awareness using something called continuous flash suppression. This technique shows participants images in such a way that they don't consciously see what those images are, they only see flashes of light. Their subconscious, however, is able to see and understand these images, and researchers can infer things from the way that participants respond to these images without even knowing. By showing participants images of naked men and women, they found that straight men tended to be repelled by images of men, gay men tended to be repelled by images of women, and straight women tended to prefer images of men while being neutral towards images of women (Lin & He, 2009). On their own, these conclusions aren't particularly exciting. But, when you consider that the participants never saw these images, or were even aware of their subconscious reactions to them, then you begin to see the importance of the subconscious mind. It influences our thoughts and behavior constantly, yet we're not even aware of it.

If you want to get the best out of your brain, you'll want to make sure you're encouraging it to be positive whenever you can. With some practice, it'll be returning the favor and you won't even notice it.

Neuroplasticity

Similar to the idea of training the subconscious is the idea of neuroplasticity—the way in which the brain changes and adapts to prioritize the things it does regularly. In short, the brain is malleable, not rigid and unchanging like a computer, and it can change and grow to do what we need it to do.

The brain is made up of neurons, nerve cells that communicate with each other and the rest of the body, processing and passing along external information. It is thought that the brain is made up of around 86 billion neurons (Herculano-Houzel, 2012), and that it is constantly changing and rewiring based on how we use it.

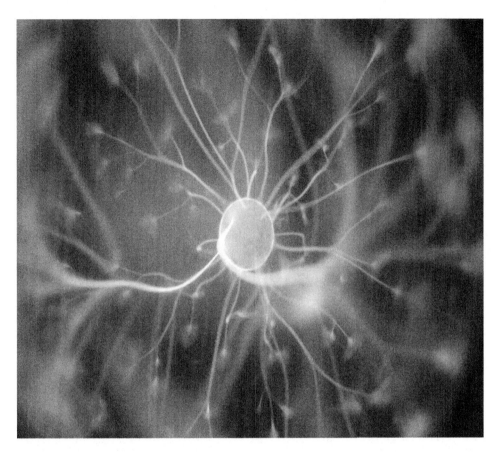

Your brain prioritizes the things that you do regularly, and it strengthens these neural pathways as a result. When people talk about the brain being a muscle you need to train, this prioritizing is the process they're referring to.

Just as the brain strengthens and reinforces important neural pathways, it also removes those we no longer use.

This process is called synaptic pruning, where the brain removes old synapses (parts of neurons used in neurotransmission) to make space for more relevant information.

The brain's adaptability is why it's so important to get into the habit of regularly practicing positive thinking.

As you do so, you strengthen the pathways associated with positivity and, when you neglect it, you run the risk of your brain deciding that maintaining the same positive synapses is inefficient and removing them entirely.

So, when you're practicing positive thought, you're literally helping to shape your brain. You might not naturally be an optimistic person, but you can teach your brain to become better at it. If you're unhappy being unhappy, just remember that you aren't stuck like that—you have the power to change.

How Emotions Regulate The State Of Mind?

Some people are naturally more emotional than others. They tend to take things to heart or wear their heart on their sleeve. Others seem to weather anything regardless of the situation. And then, there are those that simply roll with the flow of things and how they may be going. Most people tend to fall into one of these three categories. There are a few that tend to fall in between these categories and are considered to be "Grey" areas.

Sometimes mental health issues can overlap and give a person a comorbidity diagnosis. This means that the person is battling more than one of the below-listed diagnoses. They may have bits and pieces of each of the various mental health diagnoses going on simultaneously.

Learning to regulate the mind through emotions may be more challenging for some than for others. They may struggle with feelings of inadequacy or trauma. Many have struggled with mental health issues most of their lives and have found that people tend to frown on them.

Many conditions of the mind may play a role in how these people can master their thoughts. In fact, it may be more of an art for many people to master their thoughts simply.

To accomplish this, it's important to understand a few emotions or states of mind that many believe hold them back from achieving optimism. Some of these may be considered to be mood disorders or conditions, while others may simply believe it to be a state of mind.

Regardless, to achieve cheerfulness and master the art of positive actions, it's important to comprehend the meaning of these terms and how they can affect the mind's ability to be cheerful.

The Chemical Level

Going even deeper than the physical structure of the brain, let's take a moment to look at a few of the major chemicals and neurotransmitters that play a role in our mental health. When balanced, these chemicals play a significant role in maintaining a healthy mindset, and it can be useful to understand these so we know how to help maintain this balance.

Everyone has natural hormones in the body that help to regulate their mood, their perceptions, their feelings, and their health. If there is an imbalance in any of these hormones, a person may feel "Off" or "not quite themselves." Different phases of life may alter some of these hormones. For example, puberty, pregnancy, and menopause will all affect hormones in a female. In males, puberty will affect the natural hormones in the body.

Many mental health conditions require medications to help regulate how a person feels. These medications work similar to hormones and help to replace the missing chemicals in the body that may affect how a person feels, reacts, or responds to any given situation.

Oxytocin

Oxytocin is a hormone and neurotransmitter known as the love chemical due to its role in bonding. Studies have shown that oxytocin levels rise in new romantic relationships (Schneiderman et al., 2012), and are also present when mothers bond with their babies. It has even been shown that foster mothers show an increased level of oxytocin when presented with images of their foster infant, indicating that mother-infant bonding happens regardless of biological relation (Bick et al., 2012). Research suggests that increases in oxytocin, in response to parent-infant bonding, are present equally in men and women (Gordon et al., 2010).

Oxytocin also appears to play a role in pain relief. A study of fibromyalgia syndrome patients found that those who had lower levels of oxytocin tended to have higher levels of pain and stress, as well as depression and anxiety (Anderberg & Uvnäs-Moberg, 2000).

There are many ways that a person can boost the body's manufacture of oxytocin, including listening to music, yoga, getting or giving a massage, meditation, spending time with friends, spending time with pets, and random acts of kindness.

Dopamine

This neurotransmitter is made in the body and used by the nervous system to send and receive messages between nerve cells. It's often referred to as a chemical messenger. Dopamine plays a huge role in how a person feels.

Dopamine is known as the reward chemical, and it plays a role in movement, learning, memory, cognition, and emotion. Dopamine has been found to have a connection to Parkinson's Disease and depression (Bressan & Crippa, 2005), and even addiction and obesity (Volkow et al., 2017).

Dopamine's connection to addiction has to do with the 'feel-good' aspect of it. The body releases it after we engage in something that it considers to be rewarding, whether that's eating or being social.

Therefore, we build a positive association with these activities, and we are motivated to want to do it again.

It is a very complex chemical. The body will naturally release dopamine when the brain is anticipating a reward. It works on the neurological as well as the physiological functioning center of the brain. Dopamine is often altered with drug use. It alters how the brain perceives things, and many addicts struggle to stop using drugs because of how the drugs change their dopamine levels. Since dopamine is associated with how someone feels, it will ebb and flow with drug use. For those who aren't addicts, compare it to the smell of a favourite cooked meal. The mouth begins to water, and the person anxiously awaits the meal with that food.

Serotonin

Serotonin is a chemical mood stabilizer and can help to regulate and reduce anxiety and depression. It also has a role in several other parts of the body, such as the blood, bones, stomach, and intestines. A lack of serotonin is commonly associated with depression and anxiety, and it can also impact sleep.

SSRIs, or selective serotonin reuptake inhibitors, are a common type of medication prescribed to people suffering from depression or anxiety. They aim to raise serotonin levels in the body by stopping the reuptake, or absorption, of serotonin so that it stays in the system for longer.

Serotonin works on all of the body, allowing the brain cells and the nervous system cells to interact and communicate with one another. Serotonin isn't something that is found in foods. It can, however, be improved by sunlight, bright light, and exercise.

Endorphins

Endorphins are produced in the brain and throughout the body, and are known to improve mood and even relieve pain. They're produced after a range of activities, including exercise, sex, singing and dancing (R. Dunbar et al., 2012), watching something which creates a strong emotional reaction (R. Dunbar et al., 2016), eating, and laughing (R. Dunbar et al., 2011).

Endorphins are the chemical peptides that the body produces to deal with stress and pain. Endorphins are readily produced by the central nervous system and by the pituitary gland. They work on the opiate or pain receptors in the brain. In fact, endorphins are very similar to opioid drugs in that they can relieve pain and create a sensation of euphoria.

Endorphins work on the body to help regulate the appetite, reduce pain, and enhance the immune system. Many athletes will talk about a "runner's high" or how excited and euphoric they feel before or after a game. This is all regulated by endorphins. Endorphins can improve the mood and cheerfulness of a person by helping them to feel happier.

Keeping the Balance

Each of these chemicals has an important role to play in your health, both physical and mental. Unfortunately, the body doesn't always do its job perfectly, and it might need some outside assistance producing enough to maintain healthy levels. If you're just looking to give your body a little boost, there are a few simple things you can do from the comfort of your home.

Interestingly, one of the bigger factors is your diet. It has been found that there is a strong connection between the stomach and the brain, to the degree that our diet influences brain function and can even contribute to the development of mental illness (Ochoa-Repáraz & Kasper, 2016). For example, the body uses the amino acid tyrosine to produce dopamine.

It has been found that consuming a tyrosine supplement, thus increasing dopamine levels, can actually help promote deep thinking (Colzato et al., 2014). Similar research has been done with serotonin. The body makes serotonin from an amino acid called tryptophan, and, it has been found, that a lack of tryptophan in your diet can result in decreased levels of brain serotonin. The same study found that animals who had lower brain serotonin levels in the brain were more sensitive to painful stimuli, but returned to normal when provided more tryptophan (Fernstrom, 1977). You'll be pleased to know that cocoa powder and chocolate, especially dark chocolate, has been found to contain a type of antioxidant that has been shown to improve people's mood (Nehlig, 2013). Sure, it's delicious, but that's not the only reason we turn to chocolate after a bad day.

If you always seem to get a pretty serious case of the winter blues, you might actually be suffering from seasonal affective disorder. During the colder months of the year, when the days are shorter, and there is less sunlight, the body makes less serotonin, putting you more at risk of suffering from depression. It has been found that light therapy and exposure to sunlight is an effective tool for mitigating these symptoms (Harrison et al., 2015). Now, even if you don't experience seasonal affective disorder, getting a little extra sunshine during your day may be a way to boost the level of serotonin in your body—just don't forget to put on some sunscreen before heading out.

If you're low on endorphins, the easiest thing to do is head out and get a little bit of exercise. Get your heart pumping, blood flowing, and you'll be feeling better in no time! Interestingly, studies have shown that exercising in a group will see increased benefits compared to exercising alone (Cohen et al., 2009), so it could be helpful to get some friends to join you.

Being social will help you boost oxytocin levels, too. It's present during bonding, particularly between parent-child and with romantic partners, so spending time with your family or partner should give you a nice boost. As an added bonus, if your evening gets a little more interesting, oxytocin is also produced during sex and orgasms (Magon & Kalra, 2011).

If you're eating well, exercising regularly, socializing, and generally looking after yourself, your brain will probably have an easier time producing all the necessary chemicals. However, it's important to note that the best thing to do if you have serious concerns is to talk to your doctor. They'll be able to prescribe you medication if they think it's necessary, and they'll be able to give you accurate, personalized information. Being mindful of the chemical balance within your brain and body will help keep you prepared for how to deal with both the negative and positive moments in your life—and the more balance in your life the more positive thinking becomes easier to achieve.

LIVING A BETTER LIFE

3

We know that positive thinking can have a range of positive outcomes for our health. It's an important tool for living a long, fulfilling life, but it's not one that we should try to use alone. There is a range of other things we can be doing in our daily lives to improve our health and help us create a cheerful mind.

Getting Active

Looking after your body with regular exercise is an essential part of living a better life. Looking after your mind is all well and good, but it only makes up a part of you as a whole. You need to look after all of the parts of your body. Exercise has the added benefit of releasing endorphins, which boost your mood and relieve pain.

According to the Physical Activity Guidelines for Americans, more than 80% of adults and adolescents don't get enough exercise. It is recommended that adults should get at least 150 minutes of moderate exercise, or 75 minutes of vigorous exercise, every week.

Now, that might sound like a lot to try and fit into your weekly schedule, but it can be easily achieved with 30 minutes a day, five days a week. It can be as simple as going for a brisk walk at your local park or taking your bike out for a spin, but you need to get your heart pumping. One study found that after 10 minutes of moderate exercise, participants experienced increased stamina, vigor, and mood (Hansen et al., 2001). After another 10 minutes, these benefits continued and increased, but saw no more additional improvements after the initial 20 minutes. This suggests that, if you want to see the most benefits from your exercise, you'll want to do it in short bursts rather than all at once.

Managing Your Time

In this day and age, it's easy to fill your schedule and be busy from the moment you wake up until the moment you fall asleep. With the world as connected as it is, it can be hard to escape those work emails and invitations to go out for drinks. This, in itself, isn't necessarily a problem. However, saying yes to everything, never giving yourself a moment to breathe, can become a problem. We need time to rest and recharge, and it's important to make time for that whenever possible. Without it, we run the risk of being burnt out.

Burnout isn't like being tired, there's no curing this with a good night's sleep. It's a constant, pervasive feeling of complete exhaustion that affects you physically and mentally. There are several key symptoms of burnout: headaches, irritability, changes in appetite, procrastination, and even a weakened immune system resulting in more illness. It can be hard to recover from burnout once you're already experiencing it, since not many of us can just pause our lives for a few weeks while we recover. That's why, if possible, you should try to stop burnout before it happens.

Don't overload yourself. You don't need to say yes to everything, and it's a valuable skill to learn to say no without feeling guilty about it. Take time to check in with yourself and see how you're feeling every so often. If you're starting to feel a little bit worn out, it might be wise to switch out drinks with your colleagues after work for a relaxing night at home.

Don't forget to prioritize a healthy sleep schedule. It is recommended that adults get between 7 and 9 hours of sleep every night (Suni, 2021), and it can be helpful to have a set time at which you aim to go to sleep. Most people benefit from having a set routine leading up to sleep, such as reducing screen time and avoiding caffeine and alcohol. Having a well-rested brain helps promote healthy brain function, making mornings easier and ensuring that everything is running as it should be.

Being Proactive

There's nothing worse than the feeling of an impending deadline hanging over your head. Whether it's an important project for work or that slowly growing mountain of laundry in the corner of your bedroom, everyone is guilty of putting it off and saying that they'll get to it later. And sure, you probably will, but it's likely to be at the last possible minute and accompanied by a fair amount of panic. Suddenly, you'll find yourself rushing to finish everything before the deadline, and your work probably won't be up to its usual standard as a result.

Then, when it's done, you'll want to take a break and take some time to relax. After all, you've earned it! That next project can wait for a little bit, there's no rush, you've got time.

And thus, the cycle continues.

Everyone procrastinates, and, a lot of the time, we aren't procrastinating because we're lazy or have no self-control. We're doing it because of negative emotions associated with the task at hand. It has been described as putting "short-term mood repair and emotion regulation over the long-term pursuit of intended actions" (Sirois & Pychyl, 2013). We prefer to make ourselves feel better right now by putting off something stressful for later.

Having something stressful hanging over your head is no way to live, and it certainly isn't conducive to a positive, healthy life. Now and again, it can be important to sit back and take some time for yourself, but, when deadlines are looming, and you're being crushed under the weight of all your responsibilities, sometimes the best thing you can do for yourself is to sit down and get it done.

It's a common saying that "action precedes motivation," and you've probably experienced this phenomenon yourself. In many cases, the biggest challenge to finishing something is getting started, and getting over that initial hurdle can be harder than expected.

If you're struggling, take a moment to think about *why* you're struggling. Are you worried about doing a bad job and disappointing someone? Are you confused about what you need to do and don't know where to start? Once you've identified the issue, you can start coming up with a plan to tackle it. If you're worried about creating something bad, allow yourself to do a bad job.

You can improve on a first draft, but only if you have something to work with. If you're confused about where to start, ask for help. It's better to reach out and get help early than wait until the last minute when it's too late to do anything.

Getting started might be difficult, but you'll probably find that it gets easier and easier as you get into a rhythm as you work through your task. And, as you make progress and it becomes less daunting, you're lessening the negative emotions associated with it. If you want to avoid procrastination in the future, it has been found that self-forgiveness can help. One study found that students who forgave themselves over the past procrastination decreased the amount they procrastinated in the future (Wohl et al., 2010). Because the students spent time forgiving themselves, they experienced fewer negative emotions related to their procrastination, which we know to be the root of procrastination. So, cut yourself some slack the next time you catch yourself avoiding something important. .

Looking After Your Mental Health

Your mindset is hugely tied to your mental health. If you don't look after it, it can become a significant barrier to creating a positive mind. It's hard to think positively in a negative space, after all, you can walk away from a negative group of friends, but you can't walk away from your own mind.

Keep an eye on your mental health, even if you've never had any issues. Check in with yourself and reflect on how you're doing. How have you been feeling recently? Have you noticed any changes in your behavior? Are you sleeping well? Are you still excited to do the things that you enjoy? How are you coping with stress?

If you do find yourself struggling, it's more important than ever to make an effort to keep up with your positive thinking habits. By striving to create a more cheerful mindspace, you might find it easier to manage your mental health. It won't magically make your problems go away, but it will give you another tool to help keep you afloat.

Procrastination

Procrastination is putting off something that needs to be done. It's not unusual to try to tell oneself that "I'll get to that tomorrow" when in fact, tomorrow never actually gets here. When someone is constantly putting things off for another day, they're procrastinating.

There are usually four different types of procrastinators.

Avoidance

Avoiding doing something that needs to be done. No one wants to clean the bathroom, so it's avoided. No one wants to do some of the chores that are a part of daily living. It's not unusual to put these off or procrastinate.

A novelty Seeker

A person who seeks out novelty for recognition and achievement. This person may appear to be the "life of the party" at parties and other events. They readily stand out from the crowd and enjoy all of the attention that it brings them.

Self-Depreciation or telling oneself (or making sure others believe) that the person isn't good at something or good enough to be worthy of friendship or a job etc. This person may also walk around looking at the ground to avoid making eye contact with anyone.

And finally, the over-booking friend who is always "too busy" to do something, this person, is, trying to put things off that they likely don't wish to face or deal with. Overbooking is another way to procrastinate. Clearly, by overbooking, they don't have time for anyone or anything else. This procrastinates everything else in their life.

Obsessive-Compulsive Disorder

Obsessive-compulsive disorder or OCD, as it's frequently referred to, is another mental health condition that can affect people of all ages. It happens when someone is caught up in obsessions, compulsions, and other intrusive thoughts that aren't wanted.

People who struggle with obsessive-compulsive disorder may not be happy unless something specific in their life is organized. The lady who must organize her soda cans by the label's direction only to find that the tabs don't line up will be very frustrated. The child who must line all of their shoes up in the closet in a specific order will be very upset if someone messes up their orderly lineup of shoes.

Some people will compulsively wash their hands to avoid germs. All of these are types of OCD, and they may vary significantly in how severe it is for each person. OCD is treated in a variety of ways. It may be simply treated with counselling, or it may require more intervention and medication. Some will have counselling to help reduce their compulsions.

People who struggle with OCD will not be happy until whatever it is that they must reorder in their life is done to their level of perfection. They may not have to have orderliness in everything. They may only have a few things in their lives that must be ordered according to their condition.

Symptoms of OCD start slowly and may ebb and flow throughout a person's life. If the person is under stress or knows that something is about to happen, they may suddenly feel the compulsion to organize something specific to ease their stress and find happiness.

Other mental health conditions can affect a person's happiness. Not all of them are listed here. Many are in subcategories or overlap. It can be challenging at best to self-diagnose. While some are more obvious than others, it's not at all unusual for mental health issues to have a comorbidity diagnosis and run concurrently with one another.

Even if mental health conditions exist, it is possible to have a cheerful state of mind and master thoughts to create positive actions. While it may be more of a challenge, under proper medical care and therapy, they too can find joy and happiness in life and their mind.

Learning to let go of expectations and focus on positive things will go far in helping this group of people to find their joy and happiness. It's still possible to be happy and retain a happy outlook in life with such a diagnosis. By learning to avoid triggers and stressful situations, everyone can find happiness and joy in life without having to blame a medical condition on their misery.

Depression

If you're living with depression, you've likely heard your fair share of comments like "just cheer up!" or "have you tried yoga?" These comments come from a good place, but they aren't particularly helpful. If it were as easy as deciding not to be sad anymore, nobody would be depressed. Depression can make it feel like it's impossible to think positively, and, unfortunately, it's one of the times when you need positivity more than ever. The first thing to remember is that your depression isn't your fault. It can be the result of loss, or trauma, or even just chemical imbalances in the brain. You just happen to be living with it.

If you're feeling up to it, there are plenty of small things that you can do to try and incorporate some positivity into your day. Try reaching out to a friend or family member for a phone call, or even to hang out in person. Spending some time with another person can help get you out of your head, and having a laugh with a friend is always a good way to enjoy a little burst of cheer. You could try going for a walk to get the endorphins pumping, or relaxing with a funny movie and your favorite snacks.

But, sometimes, no matter what you do or how hard you try, it's impossible to break through depression's grip. Sometimes, there will be days where all you can do is lie in bed and watch the world go by. When that happens, the most important thing to remember is that you need to be kind to yourself and allow time to rest. When the worst has passed, and you feel capable of functioning again, it's time to get up and start making a plan.

First, you need to make sure that you're looking after your basic needs. Having a quick shower and putting on some clean clothes can work wonders for improving your mood, and it might give you enough of a boost to get up and start dealing with your surroundings.

If you're feeling overwhelmed and unsure of where to start, one good trick is to pick a task, such as cleaning your room or doing the dishes. Then, set a timer for five minutes and try to get as much done in that five minutes as you possibly can. By the time it's done, you might find that you want to keep going. In that case, set another timer and go again. If you don't want to go again, that's fine, too. You're still slightly closer to finishing your task, and you can always go again later.

Once you've taken care of yourself, and are no longer drowning in dirty laundry, it's time to take care of your other responsibilities. Do you have any pets or any other people who depend on you? Do you need to get any work done? If you need to, write it all out so you can see everything you need to deal with. Build up momentum by starting with the easiest one and making your way down the list. You might find that seeing them be crossed off gives you the energy to keep tackling new tasks.

Trying to use positive thinking to work through depression might feel like a bit of a waste of time as it is unlikely you can smile your way to a cure for a serious mental illness. Rather than focusing on it as a way to get rid of all your problems, look at it as a support as you deal with them.

Anxiety

It's completely normal to deal with anxiety occasionally. It's not at all unusual to be anxious before a test or a public speaking engagement. Job interviews can also be stressful and may cause someone to have anxiety. When confronted with this negative emotion, it's easy to accept this anxiety as a simple temporary situation.

Anxiety, like depression, can make it hard to see the good things in life. You might find yourself obsessed with things that could go wrong, or struggling in situations where you feel like you aren't in control.

Your mind is going a mile a minute, focusing on all these things you can't control or prevent, and there's very little room to sit down and put a positive spin on things. If you're in the middle of a panic attack, then you're probably not thinking about your morning affirmations.

It's difficult, but it isn't impossible. If you find that you're anxious about something specific, it can help to write your anxieties all down so that you can see them in front of you. Anxiety is irrational, and it doesn't hold up to scrutiny very well. Of course, it's hard to be logical when you're in the middle of a panic attack, so this kind of reflection is most effective when you're feeling calm and relaxed.

When you're feeling particularly anxious, you might find you benefit from meditation. As you focus on your breath, concentrate on slowing it down. As your breath calms, you'll probably find that your heart stops racing and you might stop an impending panic attack in its tracks. If you still find yourself anxious, or suffering from a panic attack, don't let that get to you. When you find yourself in a calmer state, it's important to be kind to yourself. It can be easy to get frustrated at yourself for seemingly overreacting to things that aren't really that bad. It's important to remind yourself that your feelings might appear out of proportion, but you're still feeling them and that doesn't make them any less important.

Anxiety often doesn't listen to reason or logic. It doesn't care that meteor-strike related deaths are so uncommon that you don't even know when the last one was, but it's still going to tell you to worry about it whenever you look up at the sky. Your anxiety isn't going to cut you any slack, so that's up to you. Have patience, keep practicing your positive thinking, and it will get easier to handle over time.

What Do Happy People Do Daily?

Some people mistakenly believe that "if only" they had "something specific," they could be happy. This couldn't be further from the truth. It's not what a person has that makes them happy. It's learning to appreciate what they do have and live in the moment—putting the focus on enjoying life where they're at.

Ever wonder why happy people are so happy? What are they doing that makes them so happy? Do they have a lot of money? Do they live in a mansion? The answers will surprise many. Most happy people are really very humble people. They may not make a lot of money. They may not live in a mansion. They may have a very humbling job. However, they've learned to be content where they're at.

Happy people are like a magnet. They naturally draw others into their circle. Everyone wants to be around someone who is happy. They "want what they have". Oftentimes, the happy person has minimal "things". They've learned to just be happy where they're at. Happy people have learned to let the little things go. They've learned to find joy in the simplest things in life.

There are many things that happy people do on a daily basis. Before a person can find true happiness, they must first understand what other happy people do daily. Here is a list of some of the things that happy people do on a daily basis. Not all happy people will do everything on this list. Some will do other things that aren't on this list; however, most of them will do a majority of these things, and they may not even be consciously aware that they're doing some of the things on the list. Some of these things may just come naturally to happy people.

1. Thankful And Appreciation

They are thankful and appreciate life. They find something each and every day to be thankful for and appreciate. Whether it is that they're thankful for a good night's sleep, thankful that they woke up, or thankful for the flowers outside, they find at least one thing to be thankful for and appreciate. By finding things to be thankful for, they are putting their focus on happiness and gratefulness.

Count blessings, not problems. Some people choose to write these things down in a journal or notebook and refer to them when they're struggling. This is a great way to remind oneself that there is goodness out there if they're feeling down or struggling to find cheerfulness as a state of mind. Some will save birthday cards, Holiday Cards, and other cards that they've been given and read over these if they're feeling down. They may have picture albums or special mementos that help remind them of happy times and bring them to the forefront of their minds frequently.

2. Let Go And Love

To let go and love, one must first forgive themselves for the past and let it go. No matter what happened in the past, today is a new day and a new beginning. For this to be effective in happiness, it's important to put it down once and for all. Learning to let go and forgive oneself and others is a major step to finding lifelong happiness.

Remember, forgiveness doesn't mean that someone has to forget what may have transpired. It simply means that the person can move on from whatever happened and acknowledge the lessons learned. Letting go is a great gift to give oneself. This one may take some practice, and it may have to be revisited frequently to fully achieve it. However, with practice, it will be well rewarded in happiness. If need be, picture locking up the memories into a vault or storage locker and then throw away the mental key.

3. Love What They Do

It's long been said that a person that loves their job doesn't work a day in their life. Of course, it's important to make ends meet and be able to pay the bills. However, that doesn't mean that a person has to be stuck in a dead-end job to accomplish this. If what they do for a living is holding them back from happiness, it's definitely time to reevaluate and find something that is more meaningful.

This may mean taking a lower-paying job for a time and going back to school. It may mean moving from a large house or apartment to a smaller house or apartment. It's well worth the sacrifice to be happy. Happy people don't need a lot to be happy. They're happy where they're at with what they have. If they don't like something about their life, they fix or repair it so that they do like it.

4. Meditation

Meditation is a way to train the mind to be more aware. To visualize better health and a sense of a more positive mindset. It's not a way to turn off the mind. It's a way to enhance the mind so that they're more able to observe what is going on around them without judging. Spending a few minutes daily meditating will go far in setting the stage for true happiness. Many famous people swear by meditation for retaining their happiness.

Many happy people take some time each day and meditate. Some who consider themselves to be very spiritual may choose to call this prayer time. Regardless of what it's called, they are taking time to reflect on what brings them peace. Happy people spend anywhere from 15 minutes each morning and evening to an hour or more daily reflecting like this. It's relaxing and brings peace and happiness.

5. Exercise

Regular exercise is vital to good health. It can release endorphins that can improve mood, and it can help to relieve stress. Exercise can be an excellent outlet for people to help improve their health and cardiovascular system. Exercise can reduce the risk of some diseases, and it can also help to boost the immune system.

Whether it's a short walk in the park, a long walk daily, or an aerobic class, happy people have found some way to exercise daily. Some people choose to exercise and wind down with some meditation. When people make these choices, the body is more energized, and people begin to feel more satisfied with their lives.

6. Affirmations

Affirmations are positive thoughts and statements that help to encourage people. They're an ideal way to overcome self-defeating thoughts and actions. They help people to change their outlook on life, improve their mood, and reduce the effects of stress on the mind and body.

Happy people often have many affirmations that they tell themselves daily. Learning to love and respect oneself will go far in helping a person to find true happiness in all that they do. A positive thought will go a long way toward happiness.

7. Smile

Happy people smile a lot. It actually takes more muscles to frown than smile, and smiling releases dopamine, which, as was discussed above, helps to improve and boost the mood. Laughing can help to release endorphins as well. All of these work together to help reduce tension and encourage a person to be happy.

Happiness releases endorphins that can improve mood. These endorphins work on the immune system and the body to improve the outlook on life. To achieve a cheerful state of mind, it starts from a simple smile and can flood through the entire being once it becomes a habit.

8. Find Joy In The Little Things

Happy people find joy in the little things. They look at the glass as "half-full" not "half-empty". They enjoy the sunrise, the sunset, the scent of the flowers that they're allergic to (just not too close to those). They appreciate that less is more. Less stress is equivalent to more happiness.

They take good care of themselves and practise self-care on a regular basis. They don't wait for happiness to find them. They find happiness and embrace it. They surround themselves with positive people. They plan to be happy on a regular daily basis, and they are.

9. Happy People Exude Confidence

Confidence is perhaps one of the most important traits of a happy person. If they're not confident, they will practise something until they are confident. Remember learning to tie shoes? Children practice this until they are confident that they can do so with ease. It takes trial and error. They may want to give up, but with persistence, they become confident that they can tie their shoes.

Happy people push past their failures and don't see limitations but rather challenges that they can overcome. They visualize their confidence and success until they succeed. They find a way to make things work and overcome challenges that prevent them from being happy.

10. Lower Expectations

When someone expects something, and it doesn't happen, they feel let down. By learning to appreciate what they do have and lower their expectations, they find happiness where they're at. Stop worrying about what others think. Twenty years from now, will it really matter?

Instead, happy people focus on the person in the mirror. Don't judge others, and avoid judging yourself. Treat mistakes as lessons learned. If it doesn't work to do something one way, then they will find another way to achieve their goal.

11. Live In The Moment

Happiness is found at the moment. Not in the past. Not in the future. In the moment. While one can remember happy things from the past and plan for fun things in the future, it's crucial to stay in the moment and treasure it.

Stay in the moment and find joy at the moment. It's amazing how happy this trait can make a person. Life is always changing, and they are grateful and treasure each moment. It's amazing how a simple walk can change the outlook on a day that seems to have gone bad. Watch a sunset, watch a sunrise, watch wildlife. Live in the moment and enjoy what life has to offer.

12. Get Plenty Of Rest

It's important to avoid getting so caught up in life that proper sleep and rest are neglected. Healthy adults require six to eight hours of sleep. Sleep is a vital part of a healthy mind and body. Most adults don't get enough rest and sleep. Even if the person is just resting, they're giving their body time to heal and rest. Rest restores energy. Often a person who isn't' happy is overtired.

It's incredible how a good night's rest of six to eight hours of quality sleep can improve a person's happiness. The body and mind do some amazing healing while resting and sleeping. Planning this time into one's day or night will go far to help them to find and achieve true happiness. When faced with a serious problem, try waiting to resolve it until a good night's sleep has been had. The outlook will be more positive and more likely to resolve itself in a positive outlook.

13. Learn Something New

Happy people learn something new each and every day. Whether they are learning how to do something new such as a craft or trade, learning a new recipe, or fine-tuning a skill that they already have, they spend at least 30 minutes a day learning something new. It can be relaxing and enjoyable to learn something new every day.

Learning something new on a daily basis helps to keep the mind sharp. It can be fun and exciting, and it can be a great way to bond with others. Bonding with others is also a great way to be more cheerful and happy. Socialization is important to good mental health. Even people who are introverts have a small circle of friends that they enjoy socializing with. Spending time having fun will release endorphins and help to improve the mood and immune system.

14. Avoid Stressful Situations

Happy people know how to avoid stress by removing themselves from stressful situations. Statistics show that stress can actually be reversed when the source of the stress is removed or reduced. Change the environment and change the outlook by removing oneself from things that don't make one happy.

On occasion, this may mean walking away from a friendship or a person that is causing them stress. Stress takes a significant toll on the body and health. It can raise a person's blood pressure, cause ulcers and other health issues, and it can rapidly deplete the immune system. Learning to avoid stress will go far to helping a person achieve a cheerful state of mind.

15. Visualize

Happy people have learned to visualize happiness. Visualize success. By focusing and visualizing on what makes them happy, these happy people are successful in their quest. Learn to look at things as "half-full", not "half-empty". Visualize the life that is desired and see the happy potential in every situation.

Visualize happiness and focus on what makes happiness. Dwell on positive thoughts and ideas. Visualizing communicates to the brain and body that they are happy. It puts the mind in a positive frame of thought and helps people to be happier. Visualization is a very valuable tool for happiness.

16. Reward Themselves

There is much to be said about reward systems. Rewards are a way of giving someone something special. Happy people have learned how to reward themselves. It may not be something that costs money. It may be something as simple as going for a walk in a special place or choosing a special dinner for that night.

There are many ways to reward oneself. Whether it's an ice cream cone, a new pair of shoes after saving for months, or some other way, happy people reward themselves and find happiness in doing so. These rewards may be very simple things—flowers, a walk, something that is virtually free yet a reward for a job well done. Rewards help keep the momentum going and encourage people to do better. Rewards release endorphins by their very act of making a person happy by the reward.

17. Happy Where They're At

There will never be a more perfect time to be happy than now. Happy people are happy where they're at. They embrace life as it comes and knows that if things aren't going their way, there is a reason, and they embrace that there is something better coming soon.

They don't dwell on negative things, such as the loss of a job. They know that a better job is just around the corner. Everything happens for a reason. They've learned to weather the storm and dance in the rain. They make the most of what they have and are happy, right where they're at.

18. Learn Lessons

Life is full of lessons, not mistakes. If no mistakes were ever made, there would be little change in the world. Happy people learn these lessons and take these lessons as ways to improve upon themselves and their situation. Making these lessons work for them and not against them improves how they feel and master their thoughts to create more positive actions and cheerful states of mind. There are no mistakes, just lessons to be learned.

Focusing on what can be learned from a mistake will prevent mistakes in the future and help to resolve the negative feeling that some mistakes can make a person feel. While some mistakes will have severe consequences, they can still be learned from, and it's possible to find happiness in the midst of life lessons learned.

19. Embrace change

Change can be frightening for many. It's easy to fall into the rut of life and find that a person feels stuck. Many people are reluctant to embrace change. It's easy to see change as a negative thing. However, change is often the catalyst to finding happiness. Change can be a good thing. It can bring fresh life into a situation. A job loss is a change. A happy person will face a job loss as an opportunity for a new and better-paying job. Change can be a good thing when it's looked at from a different perspective.

Those who have learned to embrace change are willing to take a risk and live with the consequences. Consider the person who has invested money and made a huge return on their investment. They took a risk. They embraced change and found happiness. They know that they should never invest more than they can afford to lose and have made wise decisions by accepting change. Happiness is steeped in change. Look at the sky. The clouds and sun are ever moving. Change brings about colour changes, and it can be beautiful.

20. Try And Try Again

What do happy people have in common? They never give up. Happy people never give up on anything. If they set a goal, they find a way to achieve it and they're happy doing so. They don't stop believing that they can accomplish whatever they set their minds to accomplish. They understand that it can take time to become what they want. It's like the gorgeous gardens on the magazine covers, those took time, often years, to become a reality. They didn't grow overnight. They didn't develop in one year. It took years of weeding, pruning, planting, and nourishing those gardens for them to become so beautiful.

Happy people find a way to make their happiness happen. They try a variety of techniques to achieve their goals. They keep trying and trying again until they find success. They don't listen to someone who tells them that something is impossible. If one way doesn't work, they find another. They find a way to make things happen and get the outcome that they're seeking to achieve their happiness. And, they're very successful at it.

CONCLUSION

It's clear that the power of positive thinking really can't be overstated. It'll do more than put you in a good mood, it will literally help you live longer. By having a more optimistic outlook on life and learning to better manage stress, you're even going so far as decreasing your risk of death due to disease.

The magic of positive thinking is that you don't have to be a genius, you don't have to have a fancy set-up or any expensive gear. You can do it literally anywhere, and you can do it in any way that suits you. If you're a visual thinker, you can use a journal or leave affirmations and reminders on notes across your house. If you enjoy quiet reflection, mindfulness and meditation might be more your speed. If you're a bit of a comedian, you might enjoy finding new ways to add laughter and cheer to your day. If you're most at home in the outdoors, you can always go for a run and let the endorphins do their thing.

If none of these methods work, don't be afraid to branch out and try something different. There's no right or wrong way to be a positive thinker, and there doesn't need to be a scientific study to validate your method of positive thinking. Andrew Solomon summed it up nicely in his TED talk:

If you have brain cancer, and you say that standing on your head for 20 minutes every morning makes you feel better, it may make you feel better, but you still have brain cancer, and you'll still probably die from it. But if you say that you have depression, and standing on your head for 20 minutes every day makes you feel better, then it's worked, because depression is an illness of how you feel, and if you feel better, then you are effectively not depressed anymore. (TED, 2013)

If something as odd as standing on your head makes you feel better, then it has done its job.

Once you know what makes you feel more optimistic, you need to take it from the conscious to the subconscious. Our subconscious mind is a little bit like a sponge, soaking up everything from our conscious mind. It takes in what we give it, and it influences our behavior accordingly—whether we like it or not. By feeding it a steady stream of positivity, we're setting ourselves up to enjoying the benefits of a cheerful mind even when we aren't actively feeling optimistic.

While the importance of positive thinking is clear, it's also important to remember that you, as a person, are made of many different parts. Strive for a positive mind, but don't forget that it's only one part of who you are.

You need to look after yourself physically, too. By keeping your brain and your body healthy, you're ensuring that everything is functioning well and producing all the necessary chemicals to keep you working efficiently. No amount of morning affirmations will beat a tired, neglected brain. As you prioritize time to work on your mental health, don't forget to eat well, get plenty of exercise, and maintain a healthy sleep schedule. Your mind is only one component of yourself, and it is very much at the mercy of its physical home; your body. When you fail to look after your body, and it, in turn, fails to produce everything that your mind needs to thrive, you'll find yourself struggling. But, when you ensure your physical health, as well as your mental health, that's when you begin to thrive.

Ultimately, becoming a lifelong positive thinker is the best way to see all the long-term health benefits. Anyone can become a positive thinker, no matter what stage of life they're in, but they'll only see long-term benefits if they commit to positive thinking for the long haul too. You don't need to spend an hour every day writing in your gratitude journal, but it's important not to go the other way and forget about it for months at a time.

Teaching the brain to be positive takes time, and, if we spend too much time neglecting this task, we run the risk of losing the progress we've made. Focusing on positive thought can help to strengthen the associated neural pathways, since the brain learns to prioritize them the more we use them. Conversely, if we neglect this practice, the brain may decide to remove these pathways to make room for more important information. If you want to keep prioritizing a more positive brain, you'll need to regularly make time to ensure that your brain does the same. Being a positive thinker isn't difficult. Being a positive thinker for life, however, takes dedication, and that isn't always easy.

At first, you might find that you struggle to make the time to be positive. Remember not to beat yourself up when you have bad days. Everyone has negative thoughts from time to time, and sometimes you wake up on the wrong side of the bed. The best thing you can do for yourself is to be kind. If you're dealing with depression or anxiety, you'll know that your brain isn't always the most cooperative when it comes to lightening your mood. You'll also likely know that getting frustrated with yourself doesn't help in the slightest. Cut yourself some slack, you can always try again tomorrow. You're not a failure if you're not always happy—you're human, not a robot.

But, whether positive thinking comes naturally to you, or if it's something you have to work at, hopefully you now feel confident enough to embrace it in your everyday life. With a positive mind on your side, there won't be much you can't handle.

Thank you for reading and good luck on your journey towards positive thinking.

For more information please go to this link: https://bit.ly/3vzbjSK

REFERENCES

Anderberg, U. M., & Uvnäs-Moberg, K. (2000). Plasma oxytocin levels in female fibromyalgia syndrome patients. Zeitschrift Für Rheumatologie, 59(6), 373–379.

https://doi.org/10.1007/s003930070045

Bick, J., Dozier, M., Bernard, K., Grasso, D., & Simons, R. (2012). Foster Mother-Infant Bonding: Associations Between Foster Mothers' Oxytocin Production, Electrophysiological Brain Activity, Feelings of Commitment, and Caregiving Quality. Child Development, 84(3), 826–840.

https://doi.org/10.1111/cdev.12008

Blair, I. V., Ma, J. E., & Lenton, A. P. (2001). Imagining stereotypes away: The moderation of implicit stereotypes through mental imagery. Journal of Personality and Social Psychology, 81(5), 828–841.

https://doi.org/10.1037/0022-3514.81.5.828

Bressan, R. A., & Crippa, J. A. (2005). The role of dopamine in reward and pleasure behaviour - review of data from preclinical research. Acta Psychiatrica Scandinavica, 111(s427), 14–21.

https://doi.org/10.1111/j.1600-0447.2005.00540.x

Bruna, M. (2018, January 6). [Person standing with fist raised]. Unsplash.

https://unsplash.com/photos/TzVN0xQhWaQ

Cagle, B. (2019, November 3). [Woman smiling in sunflowers]. Unsplash.

https://unsplash.com/photos/XLtWHLWuQPg

Cherry, K. (2020, September 18). Is It Possible to Overcome Implicit Bias? Verywell Mind.

https://www.verywellmind.com/implicit-bias-overview-4178401

Cohen, E. E. A., Ejsmond-Frey, R., Knight, N., & Dunbar, R. I. M. (2009). Rowers' high: behavioural synchrony is correlated with elevated pain thresholds. Biology Letters, 6(1), 106–108.

https://doi.org/10.1098/rsbl.2009.0670

Colzato, L. S., de Haan, A. M., & Hommel, B. (2014). Food for creativity: tyrosine promotes deep thinking. Psychological Research, 79(5), 709–714.

https://doi.org/10.1007/s00426-014-0610-4

Connaughton, D., Wadey, R., Hanton, S., & Jones, G. (2008). The development and maintenance of mental toughness: Perceptions of elite performers. Journal of Sports Sciences, 26(1), 83–95.

https://doi.org/10.1080/02640410701310958

Danner, D. D., Snowdon, D. A., & Friesen, W. V. (2001). Positive emotions in early life and longevity: Findings from the nun study. Journal of Personality and Social Psychology, 80(5), 804–813.

https://doi.org/10.1037/0022-3514.80.5.804

Dunbar, R. I. M., Baron, R., Frangou, A., Pearce, E., van Leeuwen, E. J. C., Stow, J., Partridge, G., MacDonald, I., Barra, V., & van Vugt, M. (2011). Social laughter is correlated with an elevated pain threshold. Proceedings of the Royal Society B: Biological Sciences, 279(1731), 1161–1167.

https://doi.org/10.1098/rspb.2011.1373

Dunbar, R. I. M., Teasdale, B., Thompson, J., Budelmann, F., Duncan, S., van Emde Boas, E., & Maguire, L. (2016). Emotional arousal when watching drama increases pain threshold and social bonding. Royal Society Open Science, 3(9), 160288.

https://doi.org/10.1098/rsos.160288

Dunbar, R., Kaskatis, K., MacDonald, I., & Barra, V. (2012). Performance of Music Elevates Pain Threshold and Positive Affect: Implications for the Evolutionary Function of Music. Evolutionary Psychology, 10(4), 688–702.

https://doi.org/10.1177/147470491201000403

Fernstrom, J. D. (1977). Effects of the diet on brain neurotransmitters. Metabolism, 26(2), 207–223.

https://doi.org/10.1016/0026-0495(77)90057-9

Gordon, I., Zagoory-Sharon, O., Leckman, J. F., & Feldman, R. (2010). Oxytocin and the Development of Parenting in Humans. Biological Psychiatry, 68(4), 377–382.

https://doi.org/10.1016/j.biopsych.2010.02.005

Grisel, J. E., Bartels, J. L., Allen, S. A., & Turgeon, V. L. (2008). Influence of β-Endorphin on anxious behavior in mice: interaction with EtOH. Psychopharmacology, 200(1), 105–115.

https://doi.org/10.1007/s00213-008-1161-4

H, Y. (2020, November 17). [Man at computer looking out window]. Unsplash.

https://unsplash.com/photos/p8DjPfqEhW0

HalGatewood.com. (2017, October 8). [Ball of electricity]. Unsplash.

https://unsplash.com/photos/OgvqXGL7XO4

Hansen, C. J., Stevens, L. C., & Coast, J. R. (2001). Exercise duration and mood state: How much is enough to feel better? Health Psychology, 20(4), 267–275.

https://doi.org/10.1037/0278-6133.20.4.267

Harrison, S. J., Tyrer, A. E., Levitan, R. D., Xu, X., Houle, S., Wilson, A. A., Nobrega, J. N., Rusjan, P. M., & Meyer, J. H. (2015). Light therapy and serotonin transporter binding in the anterior cingulate and prefrontal cortex. Acta Psychiatrica Scandinavica, 132(5), 379–388.

https://doi.org/10.1111/acps.12424

Herculano-Houzel, S. (2012). The remarkable, yet not extraordinary, human brain as a scaled-up primate brain and its associated cost. Proceedings of the National Academy of Sciences, 109(Supplement_1), 10661–10668.

https://doi.org/10.1073/pnas.1201895109

Ibrahimzade, F. (2020, November 9). [Food on table]. Unsplash.

https://unsplash.com/photos/cvvVSQp6DbM

Kim, E. S., Hagan, K. A., Grodstein, F., DeMeo, D. L., De Vivo, I., & Kubzansky, L. D. (2016). Optimism and Cause-Specific Mortality: A Prospective Cohort Study. American Journal of Epidemiology, 185(1), 21–29.

https://doi.org/10.1093/aje/kww182

Koole, S. L., Smeets, K., van Knippenberg, A., & Dijksterhuis, A. (1999). The cessation of rumination through self-affirmation. Journal of Personality and Social Psychology, 77(1), 111–125.

https://doi.org/10.1037/0022-3514.77.1.111

Kraft, T. L., & Pressman, S. D. (2012). Grin and Bear It. Psychological Science, 23(11), 1372–1378.

https://doi.org/10.1177/0956797612445312

Lally, P., van Jaarsveld, C. H. M., Potts, H. W. W., & Wardle, J. (2009). How are habits formed: Modelling habit formation in the real world. European Journal of Social Psychology, 40(6), 998–1009.

https://doi.org/10.1002/ejsp.674

Lewis, M. B. (2018). The interactions between botulinum-toxin-based facial treatments and embodied emotions. Scientific Reports, 8(1).

https://doi.org/10.1038/s41598-018-33119-1

Lin, Z., & He, S. (2009). Seeing the invisible: The scope and limits of unconscious processing in binocular rivalry. Progress in Neurobiology, 87(4), 195–211.

https://doi.org/10.1016/j.pneurobio.2008.09.002

Lopes, H. (2017, November 26). [Four people standing together]. Unsplash.

https://unsplash.com/photos/PGnqT0rXWLs

Magon, N., & Kalra, S. (2011). The orgasmic history of oxytocin: Love, lust, and labor. Indian Journal of Endocrinology and Metabolism, 15(7), 156–161.

https://doi.org/10.4103/2230-8210.84851

Matos, D. (2019, November 2). [Brain model]. Unsplash.

https://unsplash.com/photos/xtLIgpytpck

Nehlig, A. (2013). The neuroprotective effects of cocoa flavanol and its influence on cognitive performance. British Journal of Clinical Pharmacology, 75(3), 716–727.

https://doi.org/10.1111/j.1365-2125.2012.04378.x

Nohassi, M. (2017, March 29). [Silhouette of person standing with arms raised]. Unsplash.

https://unsplash.com/photos/odxB5oIG_iA

Ochoa-Repáraz, J., & Kasper, L. H. (2016). The Second Brain: Is the Gut Microbiota a Link Between Obesity and Central Nervous System Disorders? Current Obesity Reports, 5(1), 51–64.

https://doi.org/10.1007/s13679-016-0191-1

Piercy, K. L., Troiano, R. P., Ballard, R. M., Carlson, S. A., Fulton, J. E., Galuska, D. A., George, S. M., & Olson, R. D. (2018). The Physical Activity Guidelines for Americans. JAMA, 320(19), 2020–2028.

https://doi.org/10.1001/jama.2018.14854

Schneiderman, I., Zagoory-Sharon, O., Leckman, J. F., & Feldman, R. (2012). Oxytocin during the initial stages of romantic attachment: Relations to couples' interactive reciprocity. Psychoneuroendocrinology, 37(8), 1277–1285.

https://doi.org/10.1016/j.psyneuen.2011.12.021

Seaward, B. L. (1992). Humor's healing potential. Health Progress (Saint Louis, Mo.), 73(3), 66–70.

https://pubmed.ncbi.nlm.nih.gov/10116744/

Sherman, D. K., Bunyan, D. P., Creswell, J. D., & Jaremka, L. M. (2009). Psychological vulnerability and stress: The effects of self-affirmation on sympathetic nervous system responses to naturalistic stressors. Health Psychology, 28(5), 554–562.

https://doi.org/10.1037/a0014663

Simpson, E. (2016, October 25). [Woman walking along road].

Unsplash.

https://unsplash.com/photos/mNGaaLeWEp0

Sirois, F., & Pychyl, T. (2013). Procrastination and the Priority of Short-Term Mood Regulation: Consequences for Future Self. Social and Personality Psychology Compass, 7(2), 115–127.

https://doi.org/10.1111/spc3.12011

Solomon, A. (2013, December 18). Depression, the secret we share [Video]. TED Talks. https://www.ted.com/talks/andrew_solomon_depression_the_secret_we_share?language=en

Stauffer, I. (2018, March 1). [Man sitting with raised fist]. Unsplash.

https://unsplash.com/photos/bH7kZ0yazB0

Strack, F., Martin, L. L., & Stepper, S. (1988). Inhibiting and facilitating conditions of the human smile: A nonobtrusive test of the facial feedback hypothesis. Journal of Personality and Social Psychology, 54(5), 768–777.

https://doi.org/10.1037/0022-3514.54.5.768

Suni, E. (2021, March 10). How Much Sleep Do We Really Need? Sleep Foundation.

https://www.sleepfoundation.org/how-sleep-works/how-much-sleep-do-we-really-need

Volkow, N. D., Wise, R. A., & Baler, R. (2017). The dopamine motive system: implications for drug and food addiction. Nature Reviews

Neuroscience, 18(12), 741–752.

https://doi.org/10.1038/nrn.2017.130

Wilkins, J., & Eisenbraun, A. J. (2009). Humor Theories and the Physiological Benefits of Laughter. Holistic Nursing Practice, 23(6), 349–354.

https://doi.org/10.1097/hnp.0b013e3181bf37ad

Wohl, M. J., Pychyl, T. A., & Bennett, S. H. (2010). I forgive myself, now I can study: How self-forgiveness for procrastinating can reduce future procrastination. Personality and Individual Differences, 48(7), 803–808.

https://doi.org/10.1016/j.paid.2010.01.029

[Woman holding pen]. (2007, May 18). ScienceMag.Org.

https://science.sciencemag.org/content/316/5827/1002.full

Young, E. (2018, July 25). Lifting the lid on the unconscious. New Scientist.

https://www.newscientist.com/article/mg23931880-400-lifting-the-lid-on-the-unconscious/

Young, S. N. (2007). How to increase serotonin in the human brain without drugs. Journal of Psychiatry and Neuroscience, 32(6), 394–399.

https://www.ncbi.nlm.nih.gov/pmc/articles/PMC2077351/

Printed in Great Britain
by Amazon

47505708R00046